Golden Girl

Clae Crowfeld

Presentation by *BookLeaf Publishing*

Web: www.bookleafpub.com

E-mail: info@bookleafpub.com

ISBN: 9789357445337

First edition 2021

DEDICATION

To everyone who hears their own voice in these words,

you are so strong

and you are never alone.

1

From childhood to grown

from naive to learned

from rose coloured to truth

from trust to hurt

from hurt to fear

from fear to shield

from shield to strength

from violence to peace

from Golden to not

watch me grow

2

- Six years ago, where did you see yourself today?

Definitely not here

- Would you change it?

If I knew what I would have to go through, yes.

if I knew who I would become,

never.

3

With the reputation of perfection

there is no room to fail,

and there is no room to grow.

You aren't supposed to fail when you are perfect,

and if you change and grow,

you weren't so perfect after all.

(I'm tired of being Golden)

4

- How long does vivacious youth last?

As long as it takes before you see your first tragedy.

(I remember the day that my childhood died,

it was the first morning after she did.)

5

Everyone's past is littered with

coffins and broken bones

bleeding hearts and suicide notes

(I wrote a list of all the people I knew who had
depression,

I wrote too many names for only being fourteen years
old)

6

You were amazing,

but now I cringe at the thought of you

so how did we go from

wishing on shooting stars

to demons and dark memories?

(I still wish the best for you)

"Perfect" leaves no room for growth and

"Golden" is too dense to carry

leave me to evolve in peace

I don't want to fail your impossible expectations

8

You were right,

she was the sun.

but oh, Icarus

she was the kind of beautiful that your wax-coated
feathers shouldn't touch

your pride sent you soaring to her alluring light

and even though her heart was loving

your poorly crafted wings were melting

you disregarded your father's warning

and yet you have the audacity

to blame her for your fall.

9

I see you smiling, Golden girl

perfect, innocent, sweet

but I caught you pulling down your sleeves to hide the bruises on your knuckles

those broken blood vessels reminding you

that you weren't so perfect

on the night where you uncuffed your suppressed rage, anger, and fear

and you allowed them to control you, until your skin ripped and your knuckles bled

red stains left on your punching bag

you only stopped when your hands shook from adrenaline

 and the rips on your fingers stung more than the feelings you had compressed.

You liked it, didn't you?

becoming not so Golden, allowing raw human emotion
to grasp you for a moment

you liked watching blood escape your skin, proof of
your imperfections

yet you pulled down your sleeves to hide your bruised
knuckles

not letting anyone see

that you are not Golden, you are iron

a human forged into a shield with words like blades and
lips that taste of blood

yet when you see me, you smile so Golden and sweet

but that's not a smile

you're baring your teeth.

10

I don't know who you are to me

but I want you here

I want your arms around me and my head on your chest

I want to close my eyes and pretend

that our pieces fit perfectly together

but darling, I'm afraid that maybe

we aren't even from the same puzzle

11

Don't call me pretty

beauty doesn't matter.

I did not choose this body,

 it was simply given to me as a vessel for my soul

I did not choose this face,

it is simply a canvas on which to paint my emotions, not all of them picture-ready.

If you want to compliment my body,

call me strong

if you want to compliment my face,

say I'm glowing

because my flesh and bones are not for your satisfaction

they are for my function.

Quit focusing on making your body look pretty

and start beautifying your soul

because everything else is glorified dust.

13

12

I am slowly reclaiming the songs that were once ours for myself

I am slowly reclaiming all the songs that I dedicated to you.

13

It's not you that haunts me, it's your hands

they're still here from when you last touched me

severed at the wrist, they creep their way along my body,
gripping me while I try to sleep

I can't sleep

you aren't here anymore, but your hands are

they poke at me like a child with a stick pokes at a
caterpillar

I wither and curl my insect body, helpless to the giant's
will.

If I sit alone and think, your hands come and visit

stomping their hard palms along my skin as they hold
me down and re-enact what you did to me.

When he touches me it's not his hands but yours that I
feel

more coarse

more forceful

they twist his love to synthetic hunger.

Yes, your heart and your body are far gone

but I don't think your hands will ever leave me.

14

"Don't worry, I love you" said the wolf to me

as his stomach growled and he showed his teeth.

Lambs soon learn the difference between love and hunger.

15

He loved me because of my passion

he was inspired and wanted that passion too

but I need someone to match my fire, and we would burn bright into the night

feeding each other's flames

helping each other grow

I don't want someone who would take it for himself.

16

Careful, don't come too close.

I'm afraid I might mark you

- Mark me how?

The spilled ink in my heart might stain your shirt

you'll cut your soft hands on the jagged parts of me

if you kiss me too hard, you might taste poison

- I can handle the worst of you

You don't know the worst of me.

- Then let me see

- I want to see the stains on your heart

- I want to feel your rough edges

- I want to know why you have created venom to protect
yourself

Then what?

- Then I'll hold you, the whole you, poison and all.

Hold me like a burden?

- Burdens are forced

- I'm choosing to hold you, all of you.

- Let me.

17

If God put me on this earth

He did so for a reason.

And if he didn't put me here

I will find my own reason for staying.

18

You and me?

Our souls were born together

formed at the same time hydrogen, helium, and lithium
nuclei captured their electrons at the birth of the universe

you know me like you know how to breathe,

instinctively and for life

I look through your eyes and I can hear your thoughts

you hear my words and know each ounce of feeling in
my bones

not my other half (we are whole)

but the oldest companions

we knew each other before Time herself began.

19

Everything is so fucking temporary

why do people have to leave

in and out in and out

I want to hold on and not worry about when I have to let go

I want as close as I can get to a guarantee

I want you with me for as long as I can have you

I don't want to be forced to let go

but if the world is so harsh that nothing can truly remain mine forever

I want to be able to hold you at least once,

at least for a little while

20

As I toss my graduation cap into the air

I imagine you beside me

and I wonder what kind of person you would have become

if you didn't think yourself so worthless

that you stopped living at thirteen.

21

I flip to the beginning pages again

as I always do when something salient comes to an end

 I remember the girl who wrote those pages

"There are so many things I want to tell you," I think.

As my eyes dart to word after word,

I become that girl again

and she breathes deep knowing

that she doesn't have to be Golden to be satisfied.

(We were never meant to shine like gold,

but to shine like the sun and watch things grow.)